BINNING
HOUSE

ORO Editions
Publishers of Architecture, Art, and Design
Gordon Goff, publisher
www.oroeditions.com
info@oroeditions.com

ISBN 978-1-939621-66-5

10 9 8 7 6 5 4 3 2 1   FIRST EDITION

Texts by Matthew Soules
Photographs by Michael Perlmutter
Drawings by Lőrinc Vass
Series Curation by Christopher Macdonald, Sherry McKay and Leslie Van Duzer

Book design by Pablo Mandel
www.circularstudio.com

This book has been typeset in Akzidenz Grotesk.

Color Separations and Printing: ORO Group Ltd.
Printed in China

Library of Congress data available upon request. World Rights: Available
International Distribution: www.oroeditions.com/distribution

IMAGE CREDITS
All photographs by Michael Perlmutter unless noted in Appendix section.

BINNING HOUSE

MATTHEW SOULES

PHOTOGRAPHY BY MICHAEL PERLMUTTER

UBC SALA | WEST COAST MODERN HOUSE SERIES

CONTENTS

Foreword

The School of Architecture and Landscape Architecture at the University of British Columbia is committed to the documentation of significant West Coast Modern houses. As rapidly escalating land values in the Vancouver region exert enormous pressure on residences created by a postwar modernist ethos, many important houses are currently endangered. While modest in size, their significance is large. Organically integrated into their sites and constructed from local materials, these residences call attention to their region as well as their modernity. They domesticated challenging topography with innovative construction techniques and newly imagined spaces. Interiors, efficiently dimensioned to meet functional requirements, expanded to outdoor rooms won from landscaped sites. Accommodating of the car and the attendant suburban living, these modern houses configured daily life in new ways.

The residences brought together in this series were conceived in an era of economic boom, social change and a vibrant arts community that found expression in domestic construction. While they share an ethic, they are also distinguished by the specificities of their clients and the imaginative responses of their designers. Collectively, the houses, each with their own narrative, contributed to the development of a unique West Coast idiom.

Editors and curators of the series are Professors Chris Macdonald, Sherry McKay and Leslie Van Duzer. Selected authors from within and beyond the SALA faculty are as diverse in their modes of inquiry and concerns as their subjects. Funding for the series varies with each monograph and comes from a wide range of sources, reflecting the breadth of the concern for this local architectural heritage.

— Chris Macdonald, Sherry McKay, Leslie Van Duzer

Acknowledgements

There are many individuals, entities and fortuitous occurrences that bring any publication to fruition. I am honoured to have the opportunity to contribute to the West Coast Modern House Series, initiated by then SALA Director Leslie Van Duzer and curated and edited alongside Professors Christopher Macdonald and Sherry McKay. All of us interested in Vancouver's remarkable modern heritage are indebted to their leadership and hard work on this provocative series.

Lőrinc Vass, a recent SALA graduate, was invaluable in his attention to detail and the art of representation in producing the drawings that make up such an important part of the book. Professors Macdonald, McKay and Van Duzer all offered valuable editorial input. The expertise and skill of book designer Pablo Mandel and photographer Michael Perlmutter was vital. And none of this could have occurred without the generous support of the Canada Council for the Arts.

I would also like to offer a special thanks to architectural writer and curator Adele Weder who has not only been a tireless champion of the Binning House but has been a maverick at unpacking its splendours. My own understanding of the house is deeply indebted to what Weder has taught me through countless conversations and her insightful writings. Weder completed her Master of Advanced Studies in Architecture thesis at SALA on the Binning House. Her original research made the controversial, at the time, assertion that the angled walls are an integral part of the home's design. Without her primary assertion and arguments I would not be able to conceive of the house as I do today.

Lastly, I had the remarkable opportunity to live in the Binning House for five years. This allowed me to experience its qualities throughout the seasons, at all hours of the day and in a range of conditions, from midnight windstorms to serene snowy mornings. My thanks to the Land Conservancy of British Columbia and Tamsin Baker for allowing me this experience and to Professor John Bass for turning me on to its possibility.

— Matthew Soules

BCB by BCB

Introduction

Physical buildings are a common everyday experience in which the ingredients are essentially basic: roofs, walls, floors, doors and windows. This inherently quotidian character can be said to elevate the value of a modesty of means. While architectural culture has long been saturated with buildings that look impressive because of their complicated structure, form and materials, these Herculean efforts often overshadow the transformative potential of design intelligence manifest through subtle physical means. They also obscure how a building can function as a machine for producing diverse multi-sensorial bodily experiences that are also intellectually expansive. In contrast, the Binning House generates its own unique spatial world—a gentle super-reality—in which architecture traverses elemental conditions of building and life, and does so with ingenious modesty.

Bertram Charles Binning was an artist, designer and educator and one of the most influential early advocates of Modernism in British Columbia. Although Binning was not an architect, his lifelong engagement with architecture left an indelible mark on the profession. For years he taught drawing at the UBC School of Architecture. His art and design work was integrated into many prominent structures through collaborations with architects. In addition to his family home, several house designs for other clients were constructed. Through these activities and his charismatic presence in the art and architecture community of Vancouver, Binning made an outsize contribution to the design thinking in Western Canada.

Binning and his wife Jesse purchased a property in West Vancouver in 1939 and commenced design of their house shortly thereafter. While Binning authored the building's design, the task of drafting it into architectural drawings fell to his friend and collaborator, architect Ned Pratt. Construction was finished in 1941. At approximately 150 square metres, the structure is relatively modest in size. The house is composed of two simple volumes, what are effectively discrete rectangular boxes that overlap while also being offset from each other. The southern and lower of the two boxes contains a combined living and dining space at its centre. The kitchen to the east and the main bedroom to the west flank this central space. This box offers a dramatic vista overlooking English Bay, Point Grey and Vancouver Island beyond. The northern upper box, closest to the street, includes a guest sleeping space, study nook and Binning's art studio. A long and relatively narrow entrance hall occupies the location where the two boxes overlap. As an early foray in the deployment of Modernism in Western Canada, the house exhibits many of the basic tenets of the movement: flat roofs, simple rectilinear volumes, large expanses of glass and a relative absence of ornament. While operating within this common idiom, the Binning House extends Modernism's basic characteristics into conditions emerging from the particularities of the West Coast and B.C. Binning's unique preoccupations.

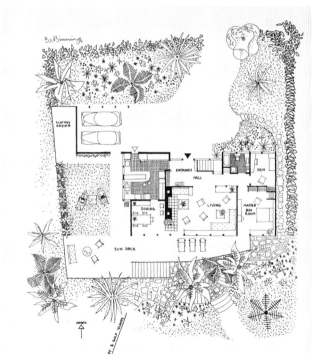

R. R. Keay House, West Vancouver. Designed by B.C. Binning.

Insides and Outsides

Perhaps the most elemental challenge of building in West Vancouver is responding to the south-facing slope that defines much of the municipality's topography. At the Binning House, this natural slope is sculpted into a series of stepping terraces, transforming rugged land into gardens and lawns. In a subtle but clever operation, the same terracing that tames the exterior runs through the interior as each of the two rectangular boxes comprising the house sits on its own terrace level. While the house is one-storey in the strict sense of the definition, a finer description accounts for its split into two interior levels in a configuration with proportions roughly matching—in both offset height and floor level width—those of the garden terraces. Indeed, the terracing operation that transforms the natural landscape is synonymous with the terracing operation that shapes the basic architecture of the house, thereby merging the constructed qualities of the exterior with the interior.

This architectural terracing synthetically yields multiple attributes. In terms of massing, it allows the house to embed itself into the site while not acquiescing to it. But it is in the coordination of movement, program and perception that the operation most poignantly functions. To enter the house, one makes a long descent from the street, passing the upper box and piercing into the lower volume where it overlaps with the upper. The sequential drop accentuates the journey into a distinct spatial environment. Since the entrance hall is located at the volumetric overlap, the floor of the lower box and the roof of the upper box define the space, resulting in the building's only over-height space. This taller space simultaneously intensifies the sense of arrival and provides a large wall surface for the display of art. Historical photos show large paintings hung within the space, conveying its use as an informal gallery for Binning's artwork. The overlapping volumes, along with their vertical offset, also allows for clerestory windows to run the full length of the hall, bringing natural light and ventilation into the centre of the house. The simplicity of the operative diagram an offset and overlap of two boxes—is ingenious for the environmental, programmatic and experiential benefits it generates.

A wall defined by ribbed glass windows separates the entrance hall from the living/dining space to its south. This interior glazing is highly unusual, even by today's standards; after all, how often does one come across windows placed within a building's interior? The uniqueness of this condition hints at its significance. Pragmatically, the glazing's translucency achieves a middle ground between separation and connection. It allows connection in the form of filtered southern light penetrating into the hallway along with subtle visual cues of that which exists beyond. It secures separation through the inherent division the wall provides.

But conceptually, the interior glazing does much more. Upon entering the inside of the building one immediately confronts the windows. It is important to remind oneself of the simple fact that windows are fundamentally a device existing at the boundary between the inside and the outside of buildings. They mediate between the exterior and the interior. The subconscious knowledge of all preceding experiences with windows inescapably informs the occupant's perception of the entrance hall space. Facing the outside of a window, the occupant is nudged into the subtle perception of having arrived inside only to still be outside. In other words, the occupant is occupying an *inside* version of the outside. When one follows the dominant trajectory of movement and subsequently passes from the entry hall beyond the threshold opening in the ribbed-glazing window wall, they enter the inside of the inside. It is not coincidental that this particular ribbed glass occurs in one other location in the house: the clerestory windows in the art studio on the northeast corner of the upper box. This clerestory is the first and only window one sees when walking from the street to the front door. With this deliberately choreographed placement of ribbed glazing, Binning is subtly preparing the subconscious with the reminder this glass belongs at the boundary between inside and outside so as to encourage the desired perceptual effect when this glass is witnessed immediately again on the inside.

Adding to the sophistication of this operation is the paradox that the inside-inside space of the house, the deep inside, is actually the single space of the house most radically open to the outside. The entire south wall of the living and dining space is floor-to-ceiling operable glass doors. In winter, the low sun streams deep into the room, as it bounces off the ocean surface into the interior. In summer, the opened doors literally merge the lawn with the interior space, creating one larger living territory where the boundary between inside and outside is erased to a remarkable degree. In this way, the deep inside is actually pretty much the outside too. When all these characteristics come into experiential focus, one can start to understand the house as a sort of machine for reappraising the purpose of architecture in the most elemental sense: to provide shelter from the exterior. At the Binning House, shelter isn't just simply provided, but rather a multiplicity of insides and outsides are perceptually produced in what amounts to an ontological meditation on the nature of being in space.

Binning painted two large murals on the house. The first is adjacent to the main entry on the exterior of the upper box and the second is at the western end of the entrance hall. The exterior mural serves as a colourful beacon, the first prominent aspect of the house viewed while descending the entry stairs. It is a destination both signifying and embellishing the moment of entry. After passing through the front door, one turns 90 degrees and moves through the long and narrow entry hall, all the while facing the second mural. The two paintings are seen in a direct sequence that aligns with movement as they act as magnets helping to choreograph an unfolding journey into the architectural environment.

The building's geometry is its most enigmatic character. Not one, but two orthogonal grids govern the planimetric orientation of walls. A primary grid determines the position of three-quarters of the walls, while a secondary grid, rotated at about five degrees from the primary, determines the position of the remaining quarter. The result is all major rooms have one wall slightly at an angle from the rest. For example, the fireplace wall in the living/dining room is not parallel with the wall across from it and does not meet its adjacent walls at 90-degree corners. Indeed, one corner is a slightly acute angle, the other a slightly obtuse angle. The fireplace wall is askew from the other three because it aligns with the secondary grid.

The entrance hall's long solid wall, opposite the ribbed glass windows, also belongs to the secondary grid. This produces the optical effect of forced perspective. Upon entering the house and looking towards the mural, the particular effect of forced perspective is foreshortening; the mind is subtly tricked into perceiving the mural as being closer than it is. In other words, the fact one long wall splays out ever so slightly has the perceptual effect of pulling the mural toward the viewer. Standing at the opposite end of the hall has the inverse effect, with the space appearing longer than it actually is. That the angled wall produces an optical effect with specific bearing on the mural wall allows the two to be understood as an operational coupling. Together they work in tandem, unifying geometry, art, optics and movement for combined effect.

Because the long wall of the hall works so closely with the mural, it is tempting to consider what correlates with the other angled walls. The primary route to move beyond the entry hall is to turn 90 degrees to the left into the living/dining room which places yet another angled wall to the right of the occupant. Unlike the entrance hall, there is no mural on the far facing wall, but another important visual destination: the natural vista. The angled wall to the right is again a device to foreshorten the visual terminus of the space, but instead of a painting, it is a large framed view that is perceptually pulled toward the occupant.

To further emphasize the optical illusions at play here, consider the building's one bathroom. Even in this small space, one of the four walls is askew, and again it is the most prominent of the four with its large mirror framed by a curious portal-like construction. This frame underscores the fact the mirror is an image—and a constructed one at that—not entirely dissimilar to a painting or a framed natural vista. The mirror and the presence of the frame amplify the angle of the wall

by reflecting the obtuse corner condition on one side and the acute corner condition on the other, producing a concave reflection in the former and a convex reflection in the latter. In this most solitary and private room, the geometric and optical methods of the house are brought into sharper focus in a manner underscoring the constructed nature of vision and space.

It is compelling to consider the character of the murals' content in relation to these operations aligning optics, art, geometry and movement. Binning did two different versions of the exterior mural over his lifetime. The interior mural, in contrast, is singular and unchanged. As a grid of repeating diamonds, triangles and circles that are self-similar but always slightly different, the interior mural presents what can be called a field condition. As a field condition, the mural is a territory defined by serial repetition in which heterogeneous diversity offers a dynamic and charged spatiality. As a painting directly on the house, this image is literally and conceptually a piece of architecture, a spatial world resonating and amplifying the spatial world of the house. Or perhaps it is a sort of cipher, where Binning's obsessions are obliquely encoded? From this second vantage, what then of the mural as a coda for the architectural plan of the house? Perhaps the house itself is a type of field condition? From this vantage, the way the house offers stability, coupled with slightly shifting dynamism, becomes more significant.

The building's materiality is a calibrated balance between locally sourced and established decorum. The interior walls are vertical tongue and groove red cedar; they have now been painted white, but were originally clear-coated to expose the wood grain. The only place the original finish remains is in the bathroom. The fireplace wall uses granite quarried in nearby Squamish. The upper box has linear Douglas fir flooring. The built-in shelving in the entrance hall is also Douglas fir. Collectively, this local wood and stone define a dominant material language of the house and convey the early interest in what has become a significant attribute of West Coast Modernism: the semiotics of local materiality. That is, the tendency of using local wood or stone in prominent locations to signify a connection to genius loci. At the same time Binning embraces local materials, he adheres to certain well-established material dispositions. While Douglas fir is the flooring in the upper box, the more public lower box utilizes oak flooring. While most built-in furnishings use local wood, those adjacent to the dining area are walnut. Both instances of non-local wood species convey the power of convention in those locations of the house where the public theatricality of domestic life is most pronounced.

The threshold between the inside and outside of the lower box, where it opens up to the garden and view, is an interesting example of the machine age opening up a new nature for domestic life. On the inside of the doors, runs a line of inset pre-cast concrete pavers, parallelograms that register the oblique angle of the fireplace wall. The glass doors literally enabling the interior and exterior to merge are prefabricated factory products said to resonate with Gropius' ideas on modern manufacturing.[1] The pavers and the doors both embody the serial repetition innate to modern manufacturing's economies of scale and foreshadow the impending dominance of modern space. Perhaps paradoxically, it is precisely these modern devices that enable architecture to shed its resolute interiority and move towards nature.

Like globally canonical modernists, such as Le Corbusier, and many other locally significant artists, Binning was interested in boats.

Ships show up frequently in his art and he and Jessie explored the coast in their sailboat, the Skookumchuck.[2] A small collection of model ships still sits in his art studio. Along the West Coast, and especially so in the early 20th century, moving by ship is the best possible way to explore the often remote splendors of coastal British Columbia. The affinity between those trying to embody the character of this part of the world in art and architecture and the sailing ship is hard to overstate. While the lifestyle of exploring the West Coast foregrounded boats, Modernist ideology also found an important quality in ships. The movement's interest in spatial efficiency found the perfect model in the design of boats in which the utility of every inch is maximized with all manner of built-in elements. From the built-in elements like the shelving and cabinetry in the entrance hall to the desk in the study nook of the upper box, the house embraces a functional utility in its architectural furnishings than can be understood in a lineage from naval architecture. The vertical tongue and groove walls add to the unmistakable nautical ambience of the house.

One of the well-worn critiques of Modernism is that it tended to devalue local particularities in favor of international values and global conditions. From this critical vantage, Corbusier's interest in ships extended directly to his buildings; many can be interpreted as floating relatively detached and disinterested in their physical contexts. Villa Savoye and Unité d'Habitation appear to be held aloft from the ground on pilotis, with the latter assuming a particularly industrial shipping-like disposition. These projects, are to many a critical gaze, too directly akin to ships that could float away to any number of possible resting points at the detriment of local culture. Of course, Modernism is an umbrella term capturing diverse strains of design, including many that resist this critique. Frank Lloyd Wright's work prominently represents one such strain.

The Binning House is clearly a structure embedded in local conditions where any interest in ships stops short of the building itself becoming an object that might float away. However, there is a distinct and powerfully diverse exploration of motion in the house. The angled walls gently destabilize the house and give it an energetic disposition. By being close to, but ever so slightly different from, conventional walls, a specific type of movement is achieved. It is a type operating both cognitively and bodily. By being just a bit off-kilter, the one-quarter of walls that are angled provoke an ongoing cognitive destabilization as the rooms perceptually oscillate between normal and exotic. This destabilization is stronger over a long duration than a dramatically non-orthogonal geometry that can be easily understood and therefore compartmentalized as being different. While the mind perpetually attempts to reconcile geometry within the Binning House, the body's normative orientation cues are also gently thrown into a similar destabilization, physically energizing the experience of the house. In these ways, the house is not so much like a ship sailing to other locations, but rather a ship at anchor bobbing up and down with the movement of the ocean. It travels while staying in place.

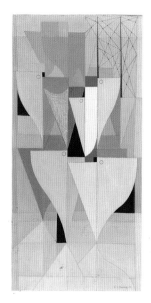

A Gentle Super-Reality

Spending time in the Binning House is like being enveloped in a gentle super-reality, not a parallel reality, but a subtle amplification or re-positioning of specific characteristics that are always, already present. This Binning House reality pivots around the concept and experience of dynamism in its multiple guises. Are the walls at an angle or not? Did one move from the inside to the outside or the reverse? What is this mural? These experiential provocations generate a deep oscillation that has the effect of emphasizing how everything is always in motion. Somehow this has a tendency to render the rustling of the Japanese maple in the garden and the shimmering of the ocean as more intense, more real: a super-reality.

It's tempting to believe the house, its surroundings and its occupants exist in some sort of resonance. The walls, the leaves and the ocean: all gently moving. Yes, this line of thinking sounds rather flaky; slipping dangerously close to something like a New Age spirituality. But there can be no doubt a deliberate act like slightly angling one-quarter of all walls was not done for its own sake as a physical condition. Frankly, as a physical condition unto itself, it's utterly unremarkable. It is not compelling to look at. It hovers between being unnoticeable and being perceived as a mistake. But it is noticeable and it's not a mistake. And because its physical fact is undeniably not its point, one must consider what it offers beyond itself. And the degree to which this type of operation can be found in the field conditions of Binning's murals and in art beyond the house only underscores his prolonged and expansive investigation. Perhaps one of the reasons why the Binning House is still so compelling almost 80 years after its construction has not so much to do with it being an originating instance of what is now known as West Coast Modernism, but rather because it manages so eloquently to produce such a timeless and elemental experience. The house is interesting because of its style, but it is magical because of the quiet movement of the world it so convincingly conjures.

Notes

1. Adele Weder, "The House," in *B.C. Binning*, eds. A. Rogatnick, I. Thom, and A. Weder (Vancouver: Douglas and McIntyre, 2006), 59.

2. Abraham Rogatnick, "A Passion for the Contemporary," in *B.C. Binning*, eds. A. Rogatnick, I. Thom, and A. Weder (Vancouver: Douglas and McIntyre, 2006), 24.

PHOTOGRAPHS

DRAWINGS

Site Plan and Section

1' 5' 10'

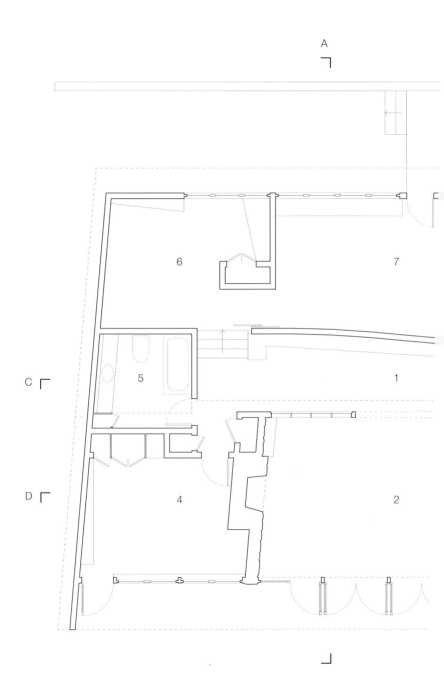

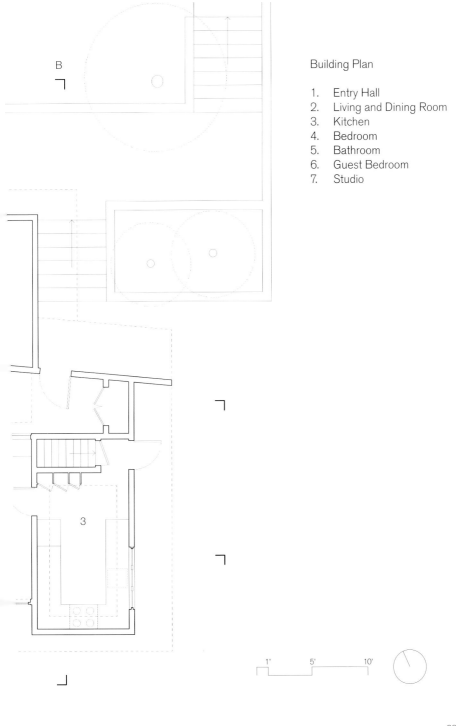

B

Building Plan

1. Entry Hall
2. Living and Dining Room
3. Kitchen
4. Bedroom
5. Bathroom
6. Guest Bedroom
7. Studio

3

1'   5'   10'

Bulding Sections A and B

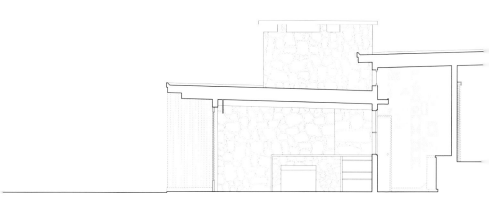

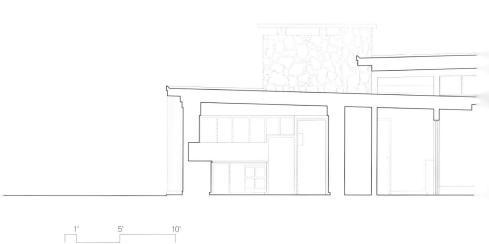

1'   5'   10'

Bulding Sections C and D

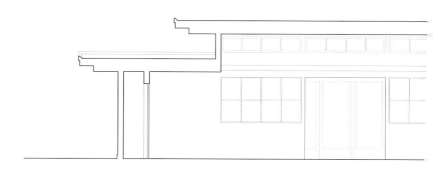

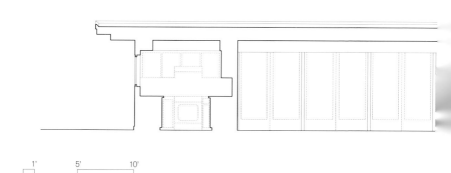

1'   5'   10'

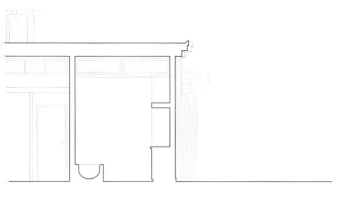

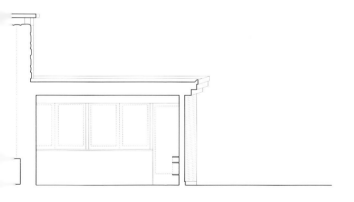

North and South Elevations

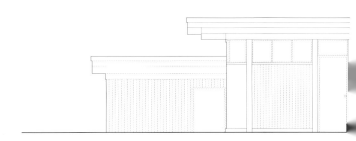

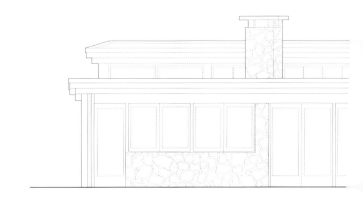

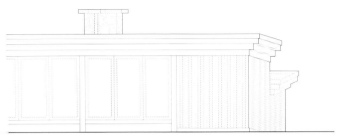

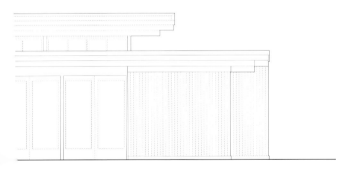

APPENDIX

Image Credits

All photographs are by Michael Perlmutter unless noted below.

Page 8: B.C. Binning, BCB by BCB, c. 1942, ink on paper, 29.3 x 21.3 cm, Collection of the Vancouver Art Gallery, Gift of Jessie Binning, VAG 2000.40.1. Photo: Trevor Mills, Vancouver Art Gallery

Page 10: B.C. Binning, Keays House Floor Plan, reproduced in "For the Keays - A Family House," *Western Homes and Living,* May 1951, p. 12.

Page 13: Graham Warrington, photographer
B.C. Binning House; ca. 1951; gelatin silver print. 18.2 x 23.9 cm; ARCH175845; B.C. Binning fonds. Collection Centre Canadien d'Architecture/Canadian Centre for Architecture, Montréal; Gift of Jessie Binning © Estate of Graham Warrington

Page 14 top: National Film Board, photographer
B.C. Binning House; ca. 1951; gelatin silver print; 19.3 x 24.1 cm; ARCH175846; B.C. Binning fonds. Collection Centre Canadien d'Architecture/Canadian Centre for Architecture, Montréal; Gift of Jessie Binning

Page 14 bottom: National Film Board of Canada, photographer
B.C. Binning House; ca. 1951; gelatin silver print; 20.32 x 25.4 cm; ARCH175849; B.C. Binning fonds. Collection Centre Canadien d'Architecture/Canadian Centre for Architecture, Montréal; Gift of Jessie Binning

Page 16: Graham Warrington, photographer. B.C. Binning in front of the house's first mural; date unknown.

Page 17: B.C. Binning, Untitled, c. 1967, oil on panel, 44.8 x 28.9 cm, Collection of the Vancouver Art Gallery, Gift of the Estate of Jessie Binning, VAG 2007.26.30; photo: Trevor Mills, Vancouver Art Gallery

Page 20 left: B.C. Binning, Untitled, 1945, ink on paper, 61.1 x 45.7 cm, Collection of the Vancouver Art Gallery, Gift of Mrs. Jessie Binning, VAG 93.46.2; photo: Vancouver Art Gallery

Page 20 right: B.C. Binning, Ships at Quiet Anchor, 1948, oil, graphite on fibreboard, 121.3 x 61.0 cm, Collection of the Vancouver Art Gallery, Gift of the Vancouver Art Gallery Women's Auxiliary, VAG 49.7; photo: Vancouver Art Gallery

Page 22: National Film Board of Canada, photographer
B.C. Binning House; ca. 1951; gelatin silver print; 20.32 x 25.4 cm; ARCH175847; B.C. Binning fonds. Collection Centre Canadien d'Architecture/Canadian Centre for Architecture, Montréal; Gift of Jessie Binning

Life and Work of B.C. Binning

1909	Born on February 19 in Medicine Hat, Alberta.
1913	Moved to Vancouver with family.
1927-32	Attended Vancouver School of Applied and Decorative Arts (renamed Vancouver School of Art in 1934 and now known as Emily Carr University of Art and Design).
1934	Appointed instructor at Vancouver School of Art.
1936	Enrolled in summer session at University of Oregon, funded by a Carnegie Scholarship (studied with Eugen Gustav Steinhof).
	Married Jessie Isabel Wylie on August 19.
1938	Studied abroad in London, England. Enrolled in classes at Central School of Art (studied with Bernard Meninsky), Westminster School of Art (studied with Mark Gertler) and Ozenfant Academy of Art (studied with Amédée Ozenfant and Henry Moore).
1940	Designed and built the Binning House.
1941	Awarded Beatrice Stone Medal for Drawing.
1944	Solo exhibition, Vancouver Art Gallery.
1946	Solo exhibition, Art Gallery of Toronto.
1949	Appointed Assistant Professor, School of Architecture, University of British Columbia.
1953	Represented Canada at the Venice Biennale (with Paul-Émile Borduas and Jean Paul Riopelle).
1955	Appointed Associate Professor and Head, Department of Fine Arts, University of British Columbia.
	First Biennial Exhibition of Canadian Painting, National Gallery of Canada.
1957	Second Biennial Exhibition of Canadian Painting, National Gallery of Canada.
1961	Appointed Professor, Department of Fine Arts, University of British Columbia.

1962	Received Allied Arts Award, Royal Architectural Institute of Canada.
1963	Awarded Canada Council Senior Fellowship.
1965	Appointed to the Advisory Panel for the Arts, Canada Council.
1968	Resigned as Head, Department of Fine Arts, University of British Columbia. Continued to teach as Professor.
1971	Appointed Officer of the Order of Canada.
1974	Retired from the University of British Columbia.
1976	Died on March 16 in Vancouver.

Book Credits

Matthew Soules author
After graduating from the Harvard University Graduate School of Design, Matthew Soules, Architect AIBC, worked for Rem Koolhaas' Office for Metropolitan Architecture in Rotterdam and Pei Cobb Freed and Partners in New York City. Upon returning to Vancouver, he founded Matthew Soules Architecture and began teaching at the University of British Columbia School of Architecture and Landscape Architecture. His research focuses on the relationship between capitalism and the built environment and extends to projects that address the architectural culture of metropolitan Vancouver. His writing has been published in journals including *Harvard Design Magazine, Praxis, Canadian Architect, Topos* and *Azure*. He has contributed chapters and essays to *Industries of Architecture, Post-War Middle-Class Housing* and *A Guidebook to Contemporary Architecture in Vancouver*. Matthew Soules Architecture has received numerous awards including the Architectural Institute of British Columbia's *Emerging Firm Award* and *Special Jury Award* in 2010 and 2015 respectively, and an *Architizer A+ Award* in the "Cultural Pavilions Category" in 2015.

Michael Perlmutter photographer
Originally from California, Michael moved to Stockholm in 1989 after completing a Master of Architecture degree at the University of California Berkeley. After practicing architecture for over twelve years in San Francisco and Stockholm, he shifted directions, refocusing on the photography of architecture, interiors and works of art. He built a broad international photography practice with a focus on the Nordic countries. Michael provided all the photographs for the book *Den Svenska Kakelugnen* (Swedish Tiled Stoves from the Eighteenth Century), which in 2007 was nominated for the prestigious August Prize, Sweden's equivalent of the National Book Award. Michael exhibits his work and teaches internationally. His work can be seen at www.archp.com.

Pablo Mandel GDC book designer
Pablo Mandel is a graphic design consultant and book designer. He has worked with some of the most renowned contemporary architects, photographers, and publishers worldwide, helping them shaping publications and communication projects. His book designs have been published worldwide and won several awards, including the Canadian Society of Landscape Architects' National Merit Award for *Grounded* (2011), and for *YUL-MTL Moving Landscapes* (2015) and the Bookbuilders West's Certificate of Excellence (image-driven trade books, 2009, 2010, 2011). Originally from Buenos Aires, Argentina, he has traveled extensively around the world. Pablo graduated from Buenos Aires University in 1995 with a degree in Graphic Design and is a Certified Member of the Society of Graphic Designers of Canada. His work can be seen at www.circularstudio.com.